What Can I Say?

What Can I Say?

How to Write Greetings
and Verse
for Every Occasion

Sadie Harris

Design Books

Designed by Karen Dangremond
Printed in the United States of America
by Edwards Brothers Incorporated

Library of Congress Cataloging-in-Publication Data
Harris, Sadie.
    What can I say? : how to write greetings and verse for every occasion /
Sadie Harris.
        p.   cm.
    Includes bibliographical references (p.   ).
    ISBN 1-55821-502-6 (cloth)
    1. Greeting cards—Authorship.   I. Title.
PN171.G74H37   1996   96-42384
808.6—dc20   CIP

Published by Design Books
Design Books are distributed by
Lyons & Burford Publishers
31 West 21st Street
New York NY 10010
5 4 3 2 1

My thanks are due to Liz Dodwell for her endless patience and ungrudging help; to Stacy Barrington for his enthusiasm and encouragement; to Nancy Green, my publisher, for having faith in me from the very beginning... and to Bestie and Fishie with my love.

CONTENTS

A Few Well-Chosen Words

How often have you tried to express sentiments on a birthday or anniversary card (or even an ordinary gift tag) that do not sound trite, insincere, or both? And how often have you been dissatisfied by what you have written—and ended up buying a ready-made, commercial greeting?

This little book is meant to help you overcome the difficulties of finding the right thing to say, so that you'll soon be able to dispense with the conventional Best Wishes stereotype message. In addition to helping you develop your own individual style, it can assist you in composing entries for contests and prizes, if you are an inveterate slogan writer; in penning personalized place cards, if you enjoy entertaining; and with a myriad other applications where a few well-chosen words can make all the difference.

Have you ever complained that you can never find a card with the right words? Well, why not have a go at composing your own?

Whether your feelings are romantic, sentimental, humorous, sympathetic, or naughty, you'll be surprised how easy it is.

Should you be more ambitious and wish to channel your efforts into a modestly profitable sideline, you can send your verses or greetings to commercial card companies. Some of these employ their own in-house writers, but names of approachable organizations can be found in such sources as *Artists and Writers Market List*, details of which are given in the Reference Bookshelf, on page 95. There is fierce competition in the field of commercial greeting cards, but the demand is there, and there's always room for a new, innovative voice. So don't be deterred. If you have something fresh and interesting to say, go ahead and say it.

If you are enterprising enough to create and design the entire card—words and illustrations—even better. For help in getting started, refer to the aforementioned Reference Bookshelf.

Whether you decide to write your greeting in verse or prose is entirely up to you. Both are appealing. Let the occasion, or your muse, decide between:

> Deck the halls with holly,
> Garland your home with love:
> Let Christmas encircle your heart
> With blessings from above.

or

May the glow from candles at Christmastime
shed light throughout the year

and

When we're together,
It's always sunlit weather;
When we're apart,
Snowflakes touch my heart.

or

Before I knew you I was lonely,
and life seemed meaningless.
Then you came along and
I began to laugh again.
You showed me just how wonderful
the world can be

It's for you to determine, poetry or prose.

When I first realized that I could convert my rhyming flair—which I had formerly used purely to amuse myself and my friends—into something marketable, I was persuaded to

send off a dozen sample verses to a greeting card company that I picked out of a directory.

Initially I hesitated, as I could not imagine that my lightweight indulgences could possibly have any commercial value. But I was wrong. Within a couple of weeks I had received a check for ten of my contributions (I still have a framed photostat copy of that first check on my wall!). Since then, I've continued to generate a small income by submitting material to companies on an irregular basis. Although you won't make your fortune this way, you'll certainly clock up a few extra dollars. All you need is a pen or pencil or access to a typewriter or word processor, a rhyming dictionary, a thesaurus, and, possibly, a dictionary of quotations.

So go to it. Remember, a word in the hand is worth two in the bush.

Tips on Writing Greetings and Verse

As I have already said, this book aims to stimulate your imagination and encourage you to draw upon easily available sources and resources to produce words that are meaningful, thus creating messages that are memorable. Following are some general tips to help you achieve this goal.

❦ Always bear in mind that the card which is a little bit different is the card that is a lot more appreciated.

❦ Try to avoid standardized wording to convey your message. One way to do this is to include something personal on the card, even if it is just the recipient's name or his or her profession or hobby. For example:

> **M**ay your path be strewn with roses and the blooms in your garden flourish (for a garden-lover)

or choose an apt quotation:

> God Almighty first planted a garden,
> and it is the purest of human pleasures.
> ("Of Gardens," Francis Bacon, 1561–1626)

❧ **Concentrate on expressive words** such as joy, warmth, friendship, love, happiness, and so on. Then get out your rhyming dictionary, juggle these words around, and you'll find that things will slot into place. If you get a couple of rhyming words in your head, as, for instance, holly/jolly, fireside/Yuletide, gladness/sadness, jot them down; then build a verse or greeting around them. For prose inscriptions, follow a similar pattern of writing down possiblities. Use a thesaurus if you like.

❧ **Be inventive.** A few simple words are invariably more effective than a labored inscription.

❧ **Keep a set of index cards** of emotive words for specific occasions that you can use over and over again when composing greetings, e.g., for **Christmas:** sparkle, tinsel, holly, snowflakes, sleigh bells; for **New Baby:** smiles, blessings, joy, treasure, and so forth. For many years I have also kept a separate list of "beautiful" words that I find charming, melodious, or that simply appeal to me personally. I am constantly adding to them.

❦ **Make a note of any quotations or sayings you come across that take your fancy, and add them to your index file. You will be surprised how useful this can be.**

❦ **If you choose to write in verse, however original or meaningful it may be, it will lose much of its effect if it does not scan properly. A verse that rhymes but is jerky and uneven sheds quite a lot of its charm and impact. Verse is actually metrical language and comprises several types of meter and units of measurement. However, as we do not propose to emulate the great poets (or even aspire to "a slim volume of verse"), we will not delve too deeply into the technicalities here.**

Various systems of visual symbols for meter have been invented, but for simplicity we will take the short curved line (◡) above a word to indicate an unaccented syllable, and a short horizontal line (–) to signify an accented one.

You will certainly agree that

◡ ◡ – ◡ ◡ –
It's your birthday today
◡ – ◡ ◡ –
So what can I say?

sounds much better than

◡ – ◡ ◡ – ◡
Today is your birthday
◡ – ◡ ◡ –
So what can I say?

This is because, although both verses rhyme, the emphasis on the three syllables at the end of the lines in the first example is the same, enabling the words to flow smoothly, while in the second verse, the emphasis at the end of the two lines differs, making the rhyme correspondingly ragged.

Read your verses aloud, then listen to where the accent or emphasis falls. Meter is of the utmost importance. Use it!

❦ As for style: you may notice that I am not a stickler for standard punctuation. The trend nowadays is to be casual in this respect.

❦ Keep a pen and notepad by your bedside in case a brilliant flash of inspiration strikes you in the middle of the night or first thing in the morning. This does happen, as I can verify, particularly if you are working on a contest entry and are still thinking about it as you fall asleep.

❦ If you decide to send material to greeting card companies, always type your contributions, double-spaced. Send them with a brief covering letter (let your work speak for itself) along the lines of the following:

"I am enclosing a selection of greeting card verses (or inscriptions, as the case may be), and would be grateful if you could let me know whether these are of interest to your organization.

"I look forward to hearing from you.
Sincerely,"

Always retain a copy of anything you submit. What doesn't appeal to one card company might well be snapped up by another.

❦ **If you go in for contests, it is worthwhile to categorize your entries—perhaps in another card index file—under such headings as Holidays, Cars, Food Appliances, Miscellaneous, and so on. Keep a note of the competition closing date; the name of the company promoting it; and the date when the prizes are actually to be distributed. This last item is very important because once the competition has closed and your entry has not been selected, you are free to reuse the rejected slogan for subsequent contests. You may well find, as I have on occasion, that a slogan that fails for one promotion will work successfully for another.**

Always complete your entry form clearly, in block letters. The judges won't waste their time wading through illegible entries, and the brilliant slogan of which you are so proud could well end up in the reject pile without ever having been looked at.

❦ Consider writing your message in a meaningful shape as a device to enliven your card presentation—for example, a Christmas tree for Christmas, or a cross for Easter:

<pre>
                A
              VERY
          VERY MERRY
          MERRY MERRY
       CHRISTMAS TO YOU
              ALL

                E
                A
                S
       G R E E T I N G S
                E
                R
                T
                I
                D
                E
</pre>

❧ An acrostic, in which, reading down, the first letter of each line spells out the recipient's name or the occasion, is guaranteed to bring special pleasure. Because they are personalized, acrostic cards are invariably a hit and well worth the small amount of trouble they take to prepare. (The fact that you can send the identical card to several acquaintances with the same name is nobody's business.)

You can use acrostics for almost any occasion: They make wonderful birthday cards and distinctive place cards at dinner. The words themselves are not so important so long as they rhyme (June/Moon is fine).

Each line should start with the appropriate initial letter—for example:

> **A**ll you need is a simple rhyme
> **C**heck around, just take your time
> **R**eally you'll not find it hard
> **O**riginality makes the card.
> **S**o, no more penning something trite
> **T**ake your time before you write
> **I**nclude ideas, concise and smart
> **C**oncentrate with all your heart.

Here are a few examples; feel free to borrow them until you get the hang of things:

Joyful greetings, skies of blue
All your wishes soon come true
May your heart be light
Each day be bright
Special love comes to you.

New days, new hopes
And memories too
No clouds to mar
Clear skies of blue
Your dearest wishes all come true.

A card to bring good wishes,
Lots of love along the way.
In all that you do
Constant and true,
Each hour should be special today.

Golden greetings,
Enjoy life anew;
Moments of pleasure,
Memorable, true
And special love I send to you.

Lines are interchangeable, as you can see, and can be adapted over and over again for different names. An odd number of lines presents no problem (as shown in James, Nancy, and Gemma). Just rhyme the last line with the preceding one or introduce a couple of short lines in the middle of the verse. (For more examples of acrostics, see Birthdays.)

Now, after digesting all this,

Go with the swim
Fly with the birds
Pen your own message
In your very own words.

Towards the end of the eighteenth century in England a book of verse appeared from which lovesick swains could make a choice of sentiments to pen to their loved ones on Valentine's Day. What to put on a Valentine is no easier today because you still might wonder how many ways there are in which to say "I Love

Valentine's Day

You." But try tying your message to something personal, like the gift it accompanies or the name of your loved one. Any tender sentiment is appropriate on Valentine's Day, or on any other day through the year for that matter.

This small bouquet comes straight
from my heart
Trimmed with a lover's knot:
It arrives with golden wishes
To the fairest flower in the plot.

or

> **T**his little gift that comes your way
> Is truly from my heart,
> It brings a tender message—
> I miss you when we're apart.

You bring meaning to my life in so many ways; not a day passes without my giving thanks for this blessing

Because of you my world has become a better place

Our love is a lifetime of magical moments

When we're apart, there's a space in my heart

Life without your love is a garden with no flowers

My life is enriched by your love

When we're together, one plus one makes one

When you speak my heart lifts; when you smile my heart sings; when we kiss my heart melts

All the beauty of the world is mirrored in your eyes

When I think of you my heart smiles

When we're together there is no need for words

You are the key that unlocks the door to my happiness

The gift of love is greater than any riches

Where you are is where I want to be

When your eyes fill with tears
my heart melts with love

If you are really stuck for something that sounds romantic, dip into literature. The works of some of the nineteenth-century poets—Browning, Byron, Keats, and Shelley—are particularly rich in loving words. And what better guaranteed-to-touch-a-loved-one's-heart words can you find than those written by William Shakespeare two centuries earlier:

Shall I compare thee to a summer's day?
(Sonnet 18)

or

Oh, that I were a glove upon thy hand
That I might touch thy cheek. (*Romeo and Juliet*)

So go ahead, line by line, and make your special Valentine, always remembering the advice of Sam Weller in Charles Dickens' *Pickwick Papers*—

"Never sign a Walentine with your name."

Easter greetings are usually either religious or fluffy-chick winsome. Here are a few samples of something different.

Endless hours of joy today
Skies of blue, no hint of gray.
Springtime sunlight,
lambkins leap,
Tender shoots begin to peep.
Easter morn, a brand-new start,
Raise your voice, lift up your heart.

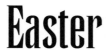

Eastertide blessings
On this holiest of days
As the light shines upon you
Give thanks and give praise.

Easter joys and Easter fun,
Painted eggs and Springtime sun:
Daffodils in golden bloom
Happy smiles light every room.

As the Easter bells ring out
Their message of hope and love,
Let joy and peace surround you
With blessings from above.

A time of new beginnings
Of joys and hopes of Spring
A time of Resurrection
That's the message that Easter will bring.

At Eastertide when the snowdrops peep
And the earth takes a whole new lease,
When leaves are unfurled,
There's hope for the world
A world filled with love and peace.

Daffodils golden
Primroses pale
Lilacs in bloom
New lambs in the dale.
Soft gentle sunshine
Skies bright and clear,
Eggs gaily painted—
Eastertide's here.

Easter brings Summer just that little bit closer

The joy of Eastertide lifts our hearts
and raises our hopes

Easter is the gateway to the splendor of Summer

Easter is the crown of Springtime

The blessings of Easter herald the
blossoms of Springtime

Easter is the curtain raiser to the Summer spectacular

**As this message you read, I don't know
Of the season (or even the date),
But I wish you a glorious Easter
Whether too early or late!**

Thanksgiving

How many of us, when sitting down to Thanksgiving celebration dinner, recall that we are commemorating 102 stalwart English Puritan separatists who crossed the Atlantic to land at Plymouth, Massachusetts, in the wintry depths of December, 1620? Perhaps still fewer realize that the reason for the customary festive turkey that graces our table is to remind us of the four wild turkeys that were served the following year at the Pilgrims' first feast of Thanksgiving for the harvest reaped by the members of the Plymouth Colony. Nowadays, Thanksgiving is usually a joyful reunion of family and friends, and you can reflect this warmth in your cards. You'll find that verses and inscriptions for Thanksgiving are easy. Just draw upon your stock of emotive words and then build on them.

May your Thanksgiving Day be a joyful reunion of loved ones and friends

Thanksgiving brings a special glow to the dusk of Autumn

May the loving warmth of Thanksgiving be with you
all through the year

      May your festive table be garlanded with
      ribbons of happiness

            May your Thanksgiving table
            be furnished with friendship
            and laden with love

      May the fellowship of Thanksgiving
      enrich every heart

On this very special day
Of loving, laughing, living,
Let every moment be enjoyed
Of your happiest-ever Thanksgiving.

      Family, fellowship, love,
      And blessings from above.
      Memories shared, jubilations—
      Happiest Thanksgiving celebrations.

Round the table smiling faces,
Turkey on display.
Friends and loved ones join together,
Giving thanks today.

On this special day in November
Let us pause for a while to remember
While our thoughts gently stray
To those far away
Let's give thanks for the caring
And the blessings we're sharing.

And let's finish off with an acrostic:

Table filled with festive fare
Happy faces, love and care
All the trimmings
Nothing missing
Kindness, laughter
Smiling, kissing.
Gathered here we all rejoice
In warmth and joy and pleasure
Voicing words from hearts so full
Invoking thoughts to treasure.
Nothing sad, no skies of gray
Giving thanks this Special Day.

Christmas

Since the very first illustrated Christmas card was produced in 1843, the traditional Yule log, carols, church bells, the jolly, and the holly have held center stage, and when verses were introduced into cards around 1870, this trend continued. (An interesting note: between 1874 and 1900, one H. M. Burnside was reputed to have penned more than 6,000 Christmas card inscriptions).

Today, Christmas cards continue broadly to conform to the family and fireside type. Your cards will benefit, however, by garlanding with a little originality. There is no denying that Yuletide, carols, and sleigh bells are evocative Christmas words, and I don't mean that you should avoid using them, but try to employ them with a touch of individuality.

Holly, tinsel, candles,
Sweet voices raised in song;
May the memories forged at Christmas
Stay with you all year long.

Christmas by the fireside—
That's the meaning of Yuletide.
Snow-capped trees by the lakeside—
That's the meaning of Yuletide.
A Ho! Ho! jolly
A sprig of holly—
That's the meaning of Yuletide.
A tall church spire,
A sweet-voiced choir—
That is the meaning of Yuletide.

> Snowflakes, holly, and mistletoe,
> The prelude to Winter's spectacular show.

I can think of no reason
For the Christmas season
The whole thing makes me sick.
If I hear one more carol
I'll go hide in a barrel
So let's get it over with—quick!

> Sleigh bells, holly,
> All things jolly, trees, and chestnuts hot.
> Tinsel, berries,
> Merry, merries
> I hate the whole darned lot!

The Christmas story can never grow old,
All through the years the tale has been told,
Of three wise men who followed the Star,
Of Joseph and Mary who'd traveled afar,
And the sweet baby Jesus asleep in the hay,
The message of old still has meaning today.

Joyful Christmas carols,
Presents 'round the tree,
Children's voices raised in joy,
Laughter, fun, and glee.

Tinsel and bells,
Roast chestnut smells,
A cheer as the last guest departs.
Everyone fed,
The children in bed—
And then the clearing up starts.

Pine trees and snow,
Small faces aglow,
Awaiting the festive dawning,
Gifts rearranged,
Greetings exchanged,
The excitement of Christmas morning.

Windows gently frosted,
Snowflakes from above,
Kinfolk, friends, rejoicing,
Sharing in the love.

On the first day of Christmas I hope you'll think of me,
On the second day of Christmas with you I long to be,
On the third day of Christmas my love is strong and true,
On the fourth day of Christmas I dream, my sweet, of you,
On the fifth day of Christmas you'll hear a robin sing,
On the sixth day of Christmas a snowdrop heralds Spring,
On the seventh day of Christmas the earth's transformed
    by snow,
On the eighth day of Christmas the winter sun's aglow,
On the ninth day of Christmas I offer you my heart,
On the tenth day of Christmas I pledge no more we'll part,
On the eleventh day of Christmas the sleigh bells sweetly
    chime,
On the twelfth day of Christmas I send my love this rhyme.

May the glow of Christmas
bring a special warmth to your heart

Let Christmas steal into your heart,
and remain there throughout the year

Birdsong is sweeter on Christmas morn

No heart is untouched by the magic of Christmas

Christmas adds a splash of color to winter

May the Christmas star light your pathway
through the darkness of winter

Christmas lights up the face of a child

May the Christmas star shine
its blessings on you

Christmas is winter's showstopper

The rose that blooms in December is more cherished
than one in June

**So pick up your snow-tipped pen, dip it in festive spirit,
and go with the flow. And if the snow happens to be lying
deep and crisp and even while you're reading this—A MERRY
CHRISTMAS TO YOU !**

New Year's greetings should be tackled quite straightforwardly. They are simply a way of conveying general good wishes.

New Year

In the year ahead
May your dreams
come true,
That's my New Year
wish for you.

May the year ahead be a great one,
And the dreams that you dream all come true:
Good health, good fortune, be happy—
My three New Year's wishes for you.

A Happy New Year
A brand-new start,
That's the wish I am sending
Straight from my heart.

The bells from the steeple are ringing,
Their message chimes out, sweet and true,
A Happy New Year
To the one I hold dear,
My love and best wishes to you.

Greetings and very best wishes,
Success in whatever you do,
May your hopes be fulfilled,
Doubts and fears all be stilled,
A Happy New Year to you!

May the coming year
Bring all you hold dear,
Good fortune, contentment, good health.
May your days bring you pleasure
In work, play, and leisure—
Of best wishes I send you a wealth.

This is the message I bring you,
A message that comes loud and clear,
For happiness, health
(And maybe some wealth)
And a bright and peaceful New Year.

May the New Year bring success
in all you strive for

A Happy New Year... and may your every hope be realized

**So, reader dear
Take it from here
Make the next twelve months
A Happy New Year!**

Although Jewish holidays are invariably strictly religious occasions, a rhyme or so, or a few personal words, would certainly not be out of place.

Rosh Hashanah, the Jewish New Year, is cele-

Rosh Hashanah

brated on the first and second days of the Hebrew month Tishri (September/October). It heralds the Ten Days of Penitence and ends with Yom Kippur, the Day of Atonement, a time of fasting and prayer for forgiveness for the past year's sins.

May the bird of peace bring freedom from strife
And your name be inscribed in the Book of Life.
    Shalom!

Three wishes I send in sincerity,
For health, for peace and prosperity.

May your New Year bring joy complete
And all that will make your life sweet.

Blessings for the New Year
for you and your family

All that is good, that is sweet, that is true—
These are my wishes for New Year, for you!
  Shalom!

> May the bird of peace bring you happiness
> in the New Year

>> In the Book of Life, may your name
>> be inscribed in gold

> May your name be inscribed in the Book of Life
> and the year to follow be a sweet one

Health and prosperity, both in good measure,
A year to remember, a New Year to treasure.

> May the year ahead
> bring everything that you hope for

>> May peace and happiness
>> surround you in the New Year

Hanukkah, a festival of lights, falls at the end of December and lasts for eight days. It is marked by the lighting of candles in a menorah (an eight-branched candelabra) to commemorate the miracle of a small vial of oil that burned for eight days.

Hanukkah

May each candle placed
in the Menorah
Bring thoughts of the
words of the Torah.

May the joy in your heart as the candles glow,
Remind you of miracles long ago.

May the candle you light today
Bring peace in your heart to stay.

As you stand in the flickering candle glow,
Remember the miracle long ago,
When oil for a day lasted eight times as long
Give thanks, count your blessings in word and in song.

Let the wonderful Season of Lights
Bring joy to the darkest of nights.

May the light from the Hanukkah candles
shine on you and your family

Passover **(March or April) recalls the exodus of the Jews from Egypt and, like Hanukkah, lasts for eight days, during which time unleavened bread (matzo) is eaten.**

Let us pray for peace among all nations and give thanks to those courageous people who continue the fight to achieve it

Passover

Let us honor those who gave their lives to build the Promised Land for us

Let us remember today all those who are still being persecuted for their beliefs

Let us pray for peace among all nations

Let us remember our ancestors who were led out of slavery that we might live in freedom

The bar mitzvah marks the initiation of 13-year-old Jewish boys into the religious community; the bat mitzvah is a similar ceremony for girls.

Bar Mitzvah
Bat Mitzvah

Now you are called to the Torah,
A milestone
of great jubilations,
To manhood from boy,
On this day filled
with joy—
An occasion for great celebrations.

Now that you've reached your Bat Mitzvah,
An exciting and wonderful stage,
Exchanging your dolls
For the great Torah scrolls,
It's the start of a wondrous New Age.

At the magical milestone in life
As the path to the future you tread,
Leaving childhood behind
Look beyond, you will find
Many years of good fortune ahead.

A milestone in life
A grand new beginning
Our pride and our hopes
On you we are pinning.

Now that you're leaving your girlhood behind,
Progressing to ventures new,
Keep faith in your heart
As you make your fresh start,
Be successful in all that you do.

Now that you've reached your Bat Mitzvah,
An exciting and wonderful stage,
No longer a girl,
From the oyster, a pearl—
The start of a wondrous New Age.

As you enter the world of an adult,
A world that's exciting and new,
Now that childhood has fled,
Life stretches ahead—
It's out there, just waiting for you!

As adulthood lies at your threshold,
And you enter a world fresh and new,
Keep faith in the teachings,
The wisdom, the preachings:
A sweet life is waiting for you.

You will find a handful of birthday greetings scattered throughout the book (for example, the acrostics in the Tips on Writing Greetings and Verse section). Let's plunge in:

Birthdays

A birthday celebration
A wonderful Special Day treat
Gifts by the score
And greetings galore
For someone delightful and sweet.

This is a day that is special,
A day of delight and rejoicing.
Happiness, fun,
A smile from the sun,
These are the wishes I'm voicing.

Birthday greetings, happiness
Blessings from above,
May your day be truly special
Brimming with joy and love.

This is the day with the golden star
This is the day when from near and far,
This is the day when good wishes are sent
From friends and from loved ones to mark the event.

And how about some acrostics: cards embodying the recipient's name are always well received:

Happy thoughts I send to you
Enjoy yourself the whole year through.
Nothing now shall make you sad
Rejoice in this, be cheerful, glad...
Your special day—the best you've had!

May your days be happy
And your heart be light,
Richness of friendship;
Your future be bright.

Pleasant thoughts
And happy dreams
Merry fun for you
Endless wishes
Love and joy
And many blessings too.

Kind thoughts and very best wishes
And love on your special day
Richness of health
Even some wealth
Nice friends, nice work, nice play.

Blessings for your special day
I'm sending greetings just to say
Lots of good things, fun and cheer
Love and joy throughout the year.

Congratulations, birthday joy,
Happy journeys far and wide;
Ambitions, hopes, good wishes
Rich dreams all realized
Leisure, pleasure, work and play
Each hour fulfilled along Life's way—
Special wishes—Special Day.

Give yourself a treat
As you turn another page
Rejoicing in the knowledge that—
You just don't look your age.

Presents, cards and greetings,
Endless time for fun;
Treasured hours for sharing with
Each and everyone.

Jeweled moments, golden wishes,
All that's bright and gay
Crown yourself because you are
King (for just one day!).

Every joy I wish for you,
Reach out and make your dreams come true.
In all the things you do, be bolder,
Cast out cares—you're one year older!

       Joy and love this special day,
       Every hour be bright and gay.
       Special thoughts
       Sincere and true
       I send you dreams both fresh and new.
       Clearest skies of brightest blue,
       All that's good, I wish for you.

**And perhaps one or two more individual greetings; you'll have
fun dreaming up some of your own along these lines, based
on the occupation (or hobby) of the recipient:**

With reference to your birthday, I'm sending volumes
of good wishes (for an avid reader)

       You've got style—you're a cut above the rest
       (for a hairdresser)

              Birthday flash: switch on to a bright
              current year (for an electrician)

I just want to say
You're my dish of the day (for someone who likes to cook)

48

W edding and engagement cards are a little tricky. The illustrations on commercially produced cards usually show only a shadowy outline of the back of the groom's head because the real-life swain could be dark or fair, short or tall, bald or long-haired—someone completely different from the illustration. The bride, of course, is another matter

Weddings & Engagements

entirely. By definition, all brides are beautiful and/or radiant, so she is invariably depicted in a cloud of frothy veiling, thereby successfully masking any distinguishing feature. As for the greeting inside the card, it consists more often than not of something along the lines of Congratulations and Best Wishes, Best Wishes to You Both, and so on. So here is fruitful ground to be original. A double acrostic—one that includes the name of both the bride and the groom—makes a clever and very welcome wedding greeting. There is also opportunity to be humorous—not to say cynical—if you wish.

May the love you share today grow still deeper in the years ahead

May the partnership of today form the union of tomorrow

A day filled with happiness—
a future filled with love

Today is the beginning
of a lifetime of love

May each day find your hearts a little closer, your
lives a little fuller, and your love a little deeper

May the light that shines on your Wedding Day
shed its glow throughout your marriage

May the links of your love be forged
in the sanctity of your marriage

May your love grow stronger
as the years grow longer

May each anniversary strengthen
the love you share today

May the romance of your Wedding Day remain with you
for the rest of your life

May flowers bloom in your hearts
for many long years to come

May your love grow and strengthen
As the years grow and lengthen.

      May your path be straight
      And your skies be blue,
      May the love you share today
      Be with you all life through.

            Best wishes on your engagement,
            I hope your future's pleasant.
            But should you decide to drift apart,
            Do please send back our present!

      On this happiest of occasions
      I'm sending all good wishes;
      Remember though, if things go wrong—
      The sea's full of other fishes.

I'm sending all good wishes
As you set out on your journey,
But should the marriage sadly fail—
My brother's a great attorney.

Best wishes, congratulations
As you travel a different course
But if things go wrong
And it seems too long
Remember there's always divorce!

Congratulations on the birth of a baby (some of these do double duty for baby showers) and baby announcements do not necessarily have to be of the "bundle of joy" type, tempting though this may be. I am a godmother several times over, and in this role have written many glowing words to proud parents. You should find no difficulty if you concentrate on those things that make a baby so cherished and special.

New Baby

The smiles of a baby shine sweet as a sunbeam; its tears are as fleeting as an April shower

A baby is the most precious jewel in the family crown

A new baby is safely enfolded by its mother's love

A baby is the pot of gold at the end of the rainbow

The shawl of a newborn babe is woven with threads of love

A baby is Nature's greatest spectacular

The home that is blessed by a baby's smile
has riches beyond compare

A baby's smile is a shaft of sunlight
after a shower of rain

The birds sing more sweetly
The world is beguiled
The stars shine more brightly
At the birth of a child.

A dapple of sunshine
A lullaby, lyrical
A handful of stardust
A baby—a miracle.

The baby that's born in the Springtime
When tender shoots peep through the ground,
Will be blessed from above,
Will bring smiles, will bring love,
And rejoicing to all those around.

Many congratulations
On the birth of your baby boy,
You've something to treasure
To bring endless pleasure
Your heart must be brimming with joy.

Congratulations, good wishes,
Your head must be in a whirl.
Your life's rearranged,
It's all been quite changed,
By the birth of your baby girl.

Congratulations on your lovely twins,
Your family circle to share.
Your joy will be double,
(They'll give you no trouble!)
This wonderful, miracle pair.

**Announcements of a baby's birth are sometimes arch,
sometimes coy, and sometimes plain statements of fact, e.g.,
Jonathan Grey, born 2/2/99; 6 lbs, 7 oz. But these are not
required forms. In most cases a dash of humor will enhance
matters considerably. For example:**

Our home is under new management—
his/her name is _____

Let trumpets play, let flags unfurl
To announce the birth of our Baby Girl.
She's delightful, she's lovely
With a smile that is sweet
Her hands are so dainty
(And also her feet).

Jonathan Grey, our newborn son
Is heaps of joy and lots of fun.
He weighs 6 pounds and his eyes are blue,
He keeps us up the whole night through.
But Jonathan Grey, our very dear son
Is greatly loved by everyone.

Or ending alternatively:

But Jonathan Grey, our blue-eyed boy
Has proved to be our favorite toy.

The following verse can easily be adapted by substituting girl for boy and she and hers for he and his:

A very dear son came home today,
He's made up his mind he's here to stay.
He's staked his claim on our hours of sleep,
(And his diaper budget's not all that cheap).
Time for ourselves is now a dream,
A moment of silence—then comes the scream.
Our very dear son came home today
And our lives have been changed—in a wonderful way.

Announcing the birth of our baby son,
Fair-haired, blue-eyed and lots of fun.

The Johnson home is filled with joy
We've a new arrival—a baby boy!

No king or queen,
No prince or earl
Can hope to compare
With our dear baby girl.

And let's finish off with an acrostic (this one for Benjamin, my own dearly loved godson):

Blessed boy, so very dear
Each tender smile, each tiny tear
New marvels daily, bringing pleasure
Joyous hours to cherish, treasure.
A new-born prince now reigns supreme
Magic milestone marks the dream
In pride of place since day of birth
No greater gift exists on earth.

Just as with cards for a new baby, it is very easy to fall into the sentimental and maudlin mode about mother and Mother's Day congratulations. I can hardly bring myself to look back on my first contributions to card companies years ago; some of them are

Mother's Day

too saccharinely awful to contemplate in the cold light of today. I blush to confess that because on many occasions I was being paid per line, I drummed up extra cash by making the verses as long as I possibly could by padding them out with the most mawkish sentiments. But that's all in the past—I'm much more selective now, and very much wiser. Let's start with a couple of literary quotations:

A mother is a mother still,
The holiest thing alive.
("The Three Graves," Samuel Taylor Coleridge, 1772–1834)

The hand that rocks the cradle rules the world.
("John O'London's Treasure Trove," William Ross Wallace, d. 1881)

When I turn to you, I smile;
When I think of you I am blessed.
Of all the mothers in the world,
I know mine is the best.

I know you're my very dear Mother,
And there's nothing, dear Mother, I lack,
Yes, I know that you care,
But I've just one small prayer—
Oh, please won't you get off my back?

No song can be sweeter
than that of a mother's lullaby to her child

The links in the chain of motherhood
are forged in the furnace of love

There is no safer haven than the shelter
of a mother's arms

No bond is stronger than that
between mother and child

The cry of a child is heard by a mother
though an ocean lie between

The humblest dwelling becomes a palace
when furnished by a mother's love

Every mother's daughter is a princess,
and every son a prince

Every mother is a lottery winner

**It is very difficult to avoid effusing or idealizing a
relationship that is often far from idyllic. But Mother's Day
is another of those instances when a certain amount of
sentimentality can be permitted without embarrassment.
So, write what you feel at the time, or what you think you
feel. The end result, although not perhaps entirely realistic,
will almost certainly be one that will bring pleasure to even
the most jaded maternal eye.**

Cards for fathers are usually much less sentimental than those destined for mothers. As long as the words convey affection and appreciation and love, there's no real problem. If you've mastered greetings for mom, this should be easy. Nevertheless, here are a few diverse ditties for dads in case you need a little help in getting started.

Father's Day

Who would be a father?
(*Othello*, William Shakespeare, 1564–1616)

> **T**here are big Dads, small Dads,
> Dark Dads and fair,
> Short Dads, tall Dads,
> Dads with no hair.
> There are dumb Dads, smart Dads,
> Dads that are divine,
> But the Dad that's best in all the world
> Is the Dad that I call mine.

Dear Dad, you're very special,
And I know that I am blessed,
It makes me glad
That you're my Dad—better than all the rest!

Dad, I love you very much
For all the things you do.
I know if I'm in trouble
I can always turn to you.
You cheer me when I'm feeling sad,
You cheer me when I'm blue,
Dad, you're best in all the world—
And that's because you're YOU!

Throughout the years you've cared for me,
And listened to my woes;
I've often seemed ungrateful,
But that's the way it goes
Now, Dad, I want to tell you,
I'd like to turn the key,
Unlock the love that's in my heart—
You mean so much to me.

A father is very special,
And you are most special of all;
You're always there when I need you,
You're always there when I call.

I'm so happy to think you're my father,
It just makes me feel very glad;
I'm sending you love that is special,
Because you're my own Special Dad.

Retirement

Retirement cards generally refer to stereotype images—carpet slippers; a watering can/gardening basket; peaceful fishing scene; an open book. No matter that the poor unfortunate recipient has never owned a pair of slippers (and certainly wouldn't dream of wearing them if he or she had); never steps into the yard except to put the garbage out; never goes near the river unless it's to cool a bottle of wine at a picnic; and prefers a round of golf to reading a book. And of course the inscriptions inside the cards are usually correspondingly unimaginative. So let's have a shot at something a little more appealing:

May your dreams become reality,
and your wishes all come true

> May retirement bring you long,
> happy years of peace and contentment

May your years of retirement be long and happy

> Wishing you a long
> and fulfilling retirement

In the years ahead may you enjoy all those things that until now
you've never had time for

A new chapter—may each page you turn
be filled with things that interest you

May each day of your retirement be rich and rewarding

Let each hour be fulfilling
Each day be well spent
And the long years ahead
Bring you peace and content.

A new phase in life is beginning
With time to unravel the thread
Time to fulfill all your wishes
And to plan for the long years ahead.

Time for friends
Time for leisure
Time to do nothing
Time for pleasure.

**I don't think you need further guidance for this one, dear
reader, so I'm retiring from the scene gracefully. Over to you
then, for something appealing, something inspiring,
something that's pleasing, for someone retiring.**

G et Well cards may be serious or humorous, depending on the situation. Naturally, you wouldn't send a card to someone at death's door telling him to stop chasing pretty nurses. But a card for a colleague, friend, or loved one absent with

Get Well

a temporary indisposition may well be of the comic type:

Hurry up and get well— you'll need all your strength to cope with the work that's accumulated in your absence

Just to keep you from feeling bored, we'll be bringing you a few little items—invoices, accounts, balance sheets, etc.

Longing for you to get back to the office— we're tired of having to do your work

Sorry to hear your system's down— hope you'll soon be up and running

Get those bugs out of your system—fast!

Hurry up and clear that virus out of your system

Please don't bother to hurry back—
We're voting on whether to give you the sack.

Get better quickly—
you're greatly missed

Please get well soon—
things just aren't the same without you

Sorry you're under the weather;
Here's a Get Well message for you—
May the sun soon shine again brightly,
And turn skies of gray back to blue.

Just as the sunshine follows the rain,
You'll soon feel fit and well again.

Obviously, words should be tailored to fit the seriousness of the illness or injury. For serious illness, keep it simple: "You are constantly in my thoughts," or "This card comes with our blessings and love," or, simply, "We miss you greatly." There is really very little that you can draw upon in these sad circumstances.

Condolence notes are arguably the most difficult of all cards to write. It is hard enough when they are addressed to acquaintances, even harder for close friends and family. But commercial condolence cards are, in my opinion, cold and insincere, displaying a lack of real emotion. A few hand-written words convey so very much more personal

Sympathy

feeling. In cases of bereavement sincerity is of paramount importance. Write what you feel and try to avoid platitudes. A personal message from the heart can make all the difference to the bereaved.

May the love of family and friends comfort you in your time of sorrow

At this time of pain and sorrow,
I would like you to know
that you are in my thoughts

Thinking of you in your sorrow and
sympathizing in your very sad loss

Your sadness and sorrow are shared by all who love you

It's sad when those whom we care for, leave,
For them, no question of choice.
And deep down inside, we silently grieve
For a still-remembered voice.
Life must go on; it is all that remains
For those left on earth below;
Try to smile, dry your tears, have courage—
You know they would wish it so.

One day the tears will cease to flow,
Another bridge will be crossed;
Then you'll recall those happy times
With one whom you've loved and lost.

When a loved one is gone
And you still carry on
With heavy and aching heart;
When a dear voice is stilled
There's a space left unfilled
In a world that's been torn far apart.
When you're left all alone
And your heart's turned to stone
And it seems that there's no one to care;
Try recalling the pleasures,
The good times, the treasures,
Find peace in the memories you share.

Your sorrow and sadness will fade with time,
Although you can never forget.
The pain and unhappiness will grow dim,
Though maybe not yet, not quite yet.

A comforting quotation can be helpful and soothing:

Better by far you should forget and smile
Than that you should remember and be sad.
("Remember," Christina Rosetti, 1830–1894)

And God will wipe away every tear from their eyes,
and death shall be no more, neither shall there be mourning
nor crying nor pain any more.
(Revelation 21:4)

Surely he has borne a grief,
And carried our sorrows.
(Isaiah, L, iii, 2)

Twilight and evening bell,
And after that the dark.
And may there be no sadness of farewell
When I embark.
("Crossing the Bar," Alfred Lord Tennyson, 1809–1892)

Friendship cards can be funny, sad, sentimental, or sarcastic. They can be written joyfully or reproachfully, or simply as straightforward greetings (acrostics, of course, are particularly apt). You can find many quotations on the subject—classical,

Friendship

biblical, and modern, under the headings "Friend" and "Friendship," from which you will be able to choose something that will fit your needs for the particular card you are sending. Or, of course, make up your own. Just use these examples to trigger ideas of your own—half the fun is in the doing.

The worst solitude is to be destitute
of sincere friendship.
("De Dignitate et Augmentis Scientiarium,"
Francis Bacon, 1561–1626)

Friendship redoubleth joys
and cutteth griefs in halves.
("Of Friendship," Francis Bacon)

A friend may well be reckoned the masterpiece of Nature.
(*Friendship*, Ralph Waldo Emerson, 1803–1882)

The only way to have a friend is to be one.
(*Friendship*, Ralph Waldo Emerson)

A faithful friend is the medicine of life.
(The Apocrypha, Ecclesiastes 6:16)

Life without friends is a garden without flowers

Friends are the bricks in the wall of life

Friends are the stepping stones
across the river of life

With you as my friend
I have riches in plenty

With you as my friend I can never be poor

Friendship is like a garden—the more work you put into it
the more you get out of it

There can be no greater comfort in life
than to reach out and grasp the hand of a friend

Cherish the flower of friendship: untended it withers and fades

The secret of friendship is caring and sharing

The doorway of friendship
is forever open

To have you as my friend
brings joy to my heart
and comfort to my soul

You are always there for me to turn to, and you never
let me down. There can be no finer friend than you

Passion brings moments of magic—
friendship a lifetime of love

A true friend is a diamond
of a thousand facets

Friendship is like a tree. Its branches offer shelter,
and the longer it stands the greater the shelter

Friendship is like a pearl—neglect it and it loses its glow

I'm here if you want me;
I'll be there if you need me

Hold fast the gift of friendship
Cherish its value and worth
With someone to share your thoughts with
You're the richest person on earth.

Through thick and through thin,
In good times and bad,
When my head starts to spin
You make me feel glad.
In heartbreak and sorrow
You remain my true friend,
There's hope for tomorrow
Right through to the end.

In my darkest hours you've a prayer for me,
My every joy you share with me,
Through thick and through thin,
When I lose, when I win,
I know that you'll always be there for me.

Throughout the years,
Through smiles and through tears,
At times when you know I'm upset
For me you are there
To love and to care—
I cherish the day that we met.

With "I miss you" and "I'm sorry" cards, you can really go to town. For these fretting and regretting occasions, no verse can be too sentimental and no words too well-used. You should have no difficulty with these cards. As usual, simply

I Miss You
I'm Sorry

write down what you think, either in prose or in verse (or adapt any of the following to your needs). From what you've absorbed in earlier chapters you should be well away.

I miss you—things just aren't the same when you're not around

Missing you . . . and remembering

I thought of you today and the world suddenly seemed a little brighter

I'm so lonely here without you

No words can express how much I'm missing you

You bring color into my life

I miss you and hope we'll be together again soon

> I miss your smile, I miss your song,
> I miss your voice so sweet and true,
> I miss the laughter and the fun
> But most of all, I'm missing YOU!

Yesterday, dear, just yesterday
You promised to be my bride;
Yesterday, dear, just yesterday
When you were close by my side.
Always, my love, I'll remember
When skies turn from blue into gray
That yesterday, dear, you answered "Yes"
So please won't you say "Yes" today?

> Every minute of every day
> I miss you so when you're away
> Every night I wish on the moon
> That you'll be back—please make it SOON!

I believe that whatever you write will achieve the desired effect. These cards are sent straight from the heart, and you can't really go wrong. The same applies to "I'm sorry" cards. Here again, almost anything you say will fit the bill. "I'm sorry—what can I do to put things right?" or "Somewhere

along the way things went wrong—I'm so sorry" or "I know I'm often thoughtless and that I hurt you. I'm sorry and I'll try harder in the future to make you happy" are simple and sincere phrases. A rhyme or so might be worth considering here, too:

> I'm sorry about the things I said
> I'm sorry I caused you pain
> What can I say, what can I do
> To make things right again?

I'm sorry I hurt you
I know I was wrong:
Take me back in your heart—
It's where I belong.

> I'm sorry I didn't say "sorry,"
> My pride just wouldn't allow;
> I didn't say "sorry" right there and then,
> So I'm saying it right here and now.

I know I've been stupid and thoughtless,
I know things I've said were quite wrong.
I do hope this won't come between us,
We've been such good friends for so long.

You must let your friends know when you move. A personal message is a lot more fun (and more memorable) than a post office address forwarding form.

In the next few days we'll be moving

Moving

(We're all in a horrible mess)
We hope very much
That you'll still keep
in touch
So here is our new address.

We're folding our tents
And moving away
(We haven't a moment to spare)
So here below is our new address—
We hope you will visit us there.

We're moving today
To another State,
Do come and see us
We can hardly wait.

The Johnson family's moving
On Thursday (that's today)
We hope you'll call and see us
Whenever you're out this way.

Or if you like a humorous edge:

We're moving today
And our spirits are thriving
If you're heading this way—
Just keep on driving!

We're moving today
(Of that there's no doubt)
If you're thinking of calling
We'll make sure that we're out!

Or even:

We're moving house today
To somewhere fresh and new,
It's worth all the trouble and fuss
Just to get away from you!

77

Send good wishes to someone who is moving, perhaps with a house-warming present:

May sunshine fill your New Home
and laughter fill your heart

New Home

May you spend
many happy years
in your New Home

May your New Home be filled with sunlight

May you find everything you desire
in your New Home

In your New Home—be happy

A fresh place to live
A Home that is new
Peace, love, and joy
And best wishes to you.

So, if you're changing your address
To a home you've just bought,
Be happy, dear reader
(Just a small, moving thought!).

Key your thank-you message to the gift or act that it acknowledges.

The flowers you sent have transformed my home into a bower of beauty

Thank You

When I look at the flowers you sent, I give thanks for your love and your kindness

A charming bouquet arrived today, It's really so lovely—what more can I say?

The flowers you sent are lovely, A beautiful bouquet; Your thoughtfulness and kindness Have brightened up my day.

Your _____ has brought me a great deal of pleasure I'll keep it for ever as something to treasure.

Thank you for the lovely _____, It's a wonderful gift that you brought. I can think of nothing nicer— It was such a delightful thought.

Thank you for the lovely _____,
Of this I'm very sure,
Your thoughtfulness and kindness
Just couldn't have pleased me more.

Your special gift has delighted me
It's a wonderful surprise,
Something I've always wanted—
A choice both thoughtful and wise.

Your kindness in sending me
such a welcome gift is so very
greatly appreciated

Your present gave me tremendous pleasure—
Thank you for your very great kindness

My day was made happy by your very special gift.
Thank you for the lovely thought

Thank you for a first-class meal
The pleasure never ceased.
I cannot praise too highly
Such a truly memorable feast.

What a glorious meal you so kindly prepared,
Each course was a special delight.
We were sad when the evening ended
And the time came to say goodnight.

Thanks for a happy occasion
Pleasant, contented, ideal:
A relaxed, enjoyable evening
And a very delightful meal.

The dinner was perfectly lovely,
The company excellent, too;
For a really wonderful evening
I send thanks and love to you.

Or just a few simple words or a quotation:

Thank you for a most charming evening.
The company was delightful
and the meal was sheer perfection

Serenely full, the epicure would say
Fate cannot harm me, I have dined today.
("Recipe for Salad," Rev. Sydney Smith, 1771–1845)

Strange to see how a good dinner
and feasting reconciles everybody.
(*Diary*, Samuel Pepys, 1633–1703)

Thank you for always being there
Whenever I'm feeling blue,
Thank you for showing how much you care—
Thank you for being you.

For your kindness and your caring
Whenever the going gets rough
For drying my tears
All through the years
I can never thank you enough.

      For your helpfulness I thank you;
      for your understanding I warm to you;
      for your kindness I love you

            Thank you for your kindness and
            understanding. Without them
            my life would be very different

      The kindness you showed me today,
      I'll remember for all my tomorrows

**Now it's time to settle down and write a few gems
of your own.**

Congratulations can be tailored for any occasion—the field is limitless. Here are a few examples.

Congratulations on taking your first steps on the path to a golden future

Congratulations

Best wishes on your promotion,
Any doubts have now happily fled,
It's not hard to tell
That you'll do very well—
Great success in the years ahead.

Many congratulations
On attaining your new position.
I know you'll succeed,
In thought, word, and deed:
You're the tops—
You've no competition!

Well done, on passing your test—
You've been so clever and smart.
I offer you congratulations,
And good wishes straight from my heart.

You've passed, well done, I'm delighted.
Your efforts have not been in vain.
Your potential you've filled,
I'm sure that you're thrilled.
Congratulations again!

Congratulations on winning the prize,
Your entry was voted the best,
You're really so smart
That I say from my heart,
You're better than all the rest.

Many congratulations,
You ran a splendid race,
A win well deserved
Your teammates you served,
You're rightly up there in first place.

There isn't much scope for originality in good wishes for those who are about to take a test, whether for a driver's license or college entrance. But if you want to cheer up someone with a hurdle coming, a few light-hearted lines never come amiss.

Exams

Don't worry, don't fret
I'm sure you will pass
Now that the Big Day is nearing,
Do your best, leave the rest
You've sure got the class—
Tomorrow we'll all be there cheering.

I know you'll do well
I know you'll excel
Just give it your best
And you'll fly through your test.

When you pick up your pen
To start your exam
To take your important test,
Please don't feel worried
Please don't get flurried
Just relax and then do your best.

I know you've worked hard
I know you're well-starred
So whatever the outcome may be,
You can hold your head high
You can reach for the sky,
Love and best wishes from me.

Don't get stressful
I know you'll be successful.

Do your best
That's all you need
Keep your nerve
I know you'll succeed.

Examinations are formidable even to the best prepared,
for the greatest fool may ask more than the wisest man
can answer.
(*Lacon*, Charles Caleb Colton, 1780?–1832)

So go ahead, now you have a try
If you don't do your best, I'll want to know why!

Entering Contests
(or, You Can Take My Words For It)

The first rule for submitting a winning slogan is to retain a copy of it. I learned this the hard way when I won a two-week family holiday to Thailand (including a personal guide and ample spending money). Everywhere we went, I was asked to recite my winning entry and I simply couldn't remember it exactly although, oddly enough, I can recall it clearly now.

How did I win? I answered four very simple questions (all answers were easily to be found within the entry form). The contest called for the completion, in not more than twelve words, of the sentence, "My family would like to visit fabulous Thailand because...."

My winning verse, which was selected by The U.K. National Film Company from 44,500-plus entries, was:

> It's romantic, exciting
> Magic and mystery,
> Exotic, beguiling
> A pageant of history

Not exactly world-shattering poetry, but it did the trick. And since finding myself in that rather embarrassing situation, I now scrupulously keep a book in which I record everything I submit.

Here are a few more of my winners. (Note that these, like the Thailand piece, cannot be reused, as they are the property of the various contest organizers who can do with them what they wish.) All of the contests imposed a limit on the number of words, which often entailed a fair amount of "weeding."

They're the best package deal
to enhance every meal
(Processed cheese products; prize £100.
Courtesy Anchor Products)

It's the bitter sweet taste that makes the sweet taste sweet
(Bitter lemon candy; prize: handsome watch. Courtesy Trebor)

Clothes, accessories, everything smart
They gain top marks, right from the start
(Back-to-school clothes;
prize: limited-edition solid brass carriage clock.
Courtesy Woolworth)

I'd outclass the rest with my golf bag
A knight in luxury armor,
With umbrella yellow
I'd be a smart fellow—
Move over, Arnold Palmer
(Soft drink/golf equipment;
prize: leather golf bag, golf umbrella.
Courtesy Schweppes/Boardroom Magazine)

When you compose a contest entry, write down your ideas irrespective of the number of words required. Your first attempts will inevitably contain more than the specified number. You should then go on to eliminate the nonessential, unimportant words, exchanging a dash for "and," substituting "it's" for "it is," and so on, until you pare it down to the necessary number. It does take a little time, and sometimes seems almost impossible, but do persevere.

Say you need a not-more-than-12-words slogan for a cruise, starting, "I would like to take my family on a cruise because…," you might come up with something like this:

There is so much to see
And so much to do
It's a treat for the children
And their parents, too

Total words: 21, but if you get to work you can prune it. Thus:

> Plenty to see
> Plenty to do
> Ideal for children
> And parents too

The original idea remains, but now it is tailored to the rules. This may take several attempts, but don't give up. Here is another sample. For a holiday slogan of not more than 24 words for a flight-plus-holiday in Malaysia, you could start off with:

> There's native art and festivals,
> colorful fabrics and flowers,
> temples, bazaars and lovely beaches.
> All this plus a dream flight to Malaysia

Although this meets the word count, it is dull and uninspiring. The salient points (taken from the entry form, which invariably contains such key data) have not been used properly. So how about:

> Folk art and festivals, fabrics and flowers,
> A colorful world of fantasia;
> Temples, tradition, fine beaches, bazaars
> A dream flight to visit Malaysia

Roughly the same number of words, but a far more attractive entry.

Now let's try a 12-words-or-less slogan for a lawn mower that is described, among other advantages in the literature, as safe, simple to use, easy to handle and maneuver. Kick around the words for a while and you might end up with something like:

Safely, simply, mowing at leisure;
Easy to handle, makes work a pleasure

Back to holiday competitions, which you might find more exciting than a lawn mower. You can juggle around any of the following to fit almost any exotic location:

Palaces, temples, and beaches,
Scenery, culture and leisure;
Bejeweled in a magical setting
A memorable Orient treasure

Temples and palaces
Breathtaking sights
Blossoms and beauty—
A land of delights

There's history, culture,
Memorable sights,
Sunshine and blossoms,
Shopping delights

There's scenery, greenery... sun for good measure,
Unparalleled beaches, unlimited pleasure

Or stun the judges with an acrostic. Here's a 30-worder for the island of Mauritius:

Mountainous splendor
And glorious scenery
Unspoiled terrain
Resplendent with greenery.
Island of beauty,
Treat for the eyes
Inlets of coral
Under tropical skies...
Stunning Mauritius—magic surprise!

Moving on to food and drink, where opportunities frequently beckon: if a competition entry starts "I like Bloggs Biscuits because..." never repeat the words "Bloggs Biscuits" in your slogan. Instead, try something like:

They're tasty, they're nourishing, pure pleasure to eat
For children and adults, a great all-round treat

It's smooth and exciting,
A great party mixer;
It's out of this world
A magic elixir

or

In the hot, dusty desert,
In the woods, by the ocean;
No drink can refresh
Like this thirst-quenching potion
(Soft drinks)

Quality, freshness
Delicious, no waste;
Value for money,
Tops for good taste
(Food products)

And commercial products, from the modest to the magnificent:

A dab on the duster
Brings out the luster

Luggage space ample
Great parking facility
Streamlined technology
Status, mobility

Tip-top technology
Touch of tradition
Beauty and flair
A car with ambition

So, pens at the ready, brains in gear, go all out for that year's supply of scouring powder (one of my own major prizes)... or perhaps a fabulous holiday or a splendid new car!

Reference Bookshelf

Making Greeting Cards
The Art and Craft of Greeting Cards. Susan Evarts. Cincinnati, Ohio: North Light Books, 1975.

The Complete Guide to Greeting Card Design. Eva Szela. Cincinnati, Ohio: North Light Books, 1987.

Tips on Making Greeting Cards. Bill Gray and Jane Van Milligen. New York: McGraw-Hill/Design Press, 1991.

Writing Advice
Writing and Selling of Greeting Card Verse. June Barr. Boston: The Writer Inc. (A series of eight occasional articles published between 1946 and 1969)

Writing Humor and Light Verse. Rosemarie Williamson. Boston: The Writer Inc., July 1993.

Writing Light Verse and Prose Humor. Richard Armour. Boston: The Writer Inc., 1980.

Source Books
Bartlett's Familiar Quotations. Boston: Little Brown and Company, 1992.

English Romantic Verse. New York: Viking Penguin, 1968.

The Home Book of Shakespeare Quotations. New York: Charles Scribner's Sons, 1937. (A concordance and glossary of unique words and phrases in Shakespeare's plays and poems.)

Merriam-Webster's Rhyming Dictionary. Springfield, Massachusetts: Merriam-Webster, Inc., 1995.

The New Oxford Annotated Bible, Revised Standard Version. New York: Oxford University Press, 1977.

The Riverside Shakespeare. Boston: Houghton Mifflin, 1974.

Roget's International Thesaurus. New York: HarperCollins Publishers Inc., 1992. Also in paper: Harper Paperback Books, 1994.

Selling Your Work

Artists and Writers Market List. Washington, D.C.: Greeting Card Creative Network's Artists & Writers Market List, Greeting Card Assn., 1991.

Writers' and Artists' Yearbook. London: A. & C. Black, 1992.

Miscellaneous

The Romance of Greeting Cards. Ernest D. Chase. Detroit: Tower Books, 1971.

And do bear in mind that a visit to your local library can prove richly rewarding.

BAKER & TAYLOR